PRAISE FOR BALTIMORE BITES & VONNA WEEKLY

"Vonna's Christmas Eve open houses were always amazing—foods I have never tried before, but were always delicious. I looked forward to it every year."

CHRIS SCHILLING
Parkton, MD

"I love the variety of pasta and assortment of appetizers. Her broccoli and chicken pasta is the best!"

LAURIE DUDEK
Parkville, MD

"You can taste the love in Vonna's culinary creations."

MARY SNYDER
Dundalk, MD

"Every dish Vonna made was a wonderful and adventurous experience in the uniqueness of the dish and the taste. It's nothing like I have experienced before."

JIM BOYCE
Wilson Point, MD

"Vonna sets a wonderful Christmas table, not only decorative but has many delicious dishes. I looked forward for many years to going to her Christmas Eve Party and I hated when she moved away."

BILL HINZMAN
Baltimore, MD

BALTIMORE BITES

A Taste from Home

VONNA R. WEEKLY

Front Cover Artwork by Emily Seminazzi-Griffin

Other Artwork by Alicia Davis

Cover & Interior Design by Imagine! Studios, LLC
www.ArtsImagine.com

Published by V52 Publications
Greensboro, North Carolina

ISBN 13: 978-0-9835763-0-3

Library of Congress Control Number: 2012955828

First V52 Publications printing: January 2013

TABLE OF CONTENTS

ACKNOWLEDGEMENTS

I want to thank God for giving me the vision for this book and for putting the right people in place to see it through. I thank Him for giving me not just the gift of cooking, but the joy that comes along with it. "With God, all things are possible."

This book is dedicated to the first person I ever cooked for, my dad—James Weekly. He ate everything and anything I made from the time I was eight years old, including all of my experiments. He would graciously smile and encourage me as he asked for a drink. He was my incentive to cook; those moments together have created memories that I will always treasure. Thanks Weiselpuss.

I also want to give credit to all of my Christmas Eve friends, both old and new, who showed up every year for 25 years to sample my food.

Last but not least I want to thank my daughter Emily. She grew up eating vegan, vegetarian, and meat dishes. She loved most of them, but I appreciate and thank her for her honesty when it just wasn't good. Her requests for me to "work my magic" when she needed help in the kitchen or when her friends were coming over were uplifting and appreciated. I thank her for her patience and encouragement.

I would also like to thank the following:

Doug Gueydan—Sponsorship
Megan Lease—Editor
Kristen Eckstein—Ultimate Book Coach

INTRODUCTION

I believe the recipes in *Baltimore Bites* will bring enjoyment to anyone who picks it up. Containing easy and non- “fru fru” recipes, this is a cookbook that both novice and experienced chefs can enjoy.

The foods listed in this book have been popular requests from friends and family for over 25 years. Starting with just a few appetizers on Christmas Eve with my mom and newborn daughter, I invited a few neighbors by to enjoy Christmas cheer… and so it began. As word spread, my Christmas Eve open house began to snowball. What once started as s simple spread with a few appetizers turned into years of gourmet feasts with demands to bring back foods served in previous years.

This book is special to me because it was written from my heart. Each recipe holds a very special memory from years of entertaining and events. It warms my heart to see my guests enjoy and delight in anticipating what new additions I'll prepare along with my tried-and-true annual foods.

No one ever leaves my home hungry. There is something for everyone.

Vonna Weekly
“A Dreamer Lives Forever”

Please note that a percentage of the sales from each and every book sold will be donated to Animal Rescue throughout the United States.

ABOUT VONNA

Vonna Weekly is a native of Baltimore, Maryland. After her company closed in 2008 and she was unable to secure steady employment, Vonna jumped at the opportunity to move to High Point, NC to be with her daughter for the birth of her first Grandpuddin, Kayden. With work still sparse and unemployment high, she decided to go to college at 50 years old. It was during this time that she became enthusiastic about the idea of putting her passion into action. Missing food from home and her friends to share it with, *Baltimore Bites: A Taste From Home* was born.

At the time of publishing, Vonna now has a second Grandpuddin, Jacob. She is due to graduate in the Fall of 2013 with a degree in Medical Office Administration. In her free time, Vonna spends every chance she gets with her two Grandpuddins and her daughter. She is an animal rights activist and also enjoys walks with her 13 ½-year-old lab Buster, reading, exercise, and of course, creating new recipes and cooking for her new friends and gatherings.

APPETIZERS

"Bean there, dipped that!"

FETA DIP

- ¾ c. feta cheese, crumbled
- ½ c. mayonnaise
- ¼ c. grated Parmesan cheese
- 2-oz. jar pimentos, drained and diced
- 2 garlic cloves, minced
- 3 drops of Tabasco sauce

Preheat oven to 350°. Thoroughly mix feta, mayonnaise, Parmesan, pimentos, garlic, and Tabasco in a casserole dish. Bake uncovered 25 minutes or until brown.

Serve with Melba toast or your favorite cracker.

GLAZED MEATBALLS

- 12- to 16- oz. bag frozen meatballs, precooked
- 12 oz. chili sauce
- 12-oz. jar grape jam

Mix together chili sauce and grape jelly. Put mixture in a Crock-Pot; add meatballs. Cook on low until heated through and sauce has thickened, approximately 30–45 minutes.

BAKED BRIE

1 large Brie wheel
6- to 8- oz. jar of jam, any flavor (I recommend raspberry)
8 oz. walnuts, chopped
1 sheet puff pastry dough, thawed

Preheat oven to 350°. Lay dough out flat. Spread jam over dough. Spread chopped walnuts over jam. Cut the rind off of the Brie wheel. Place entire wheel on top of walnuts, jam, and dough. If desired, top Brie with more walnuts and jam. Wrap dough around Brie and tuck corners in tight. Bake 40 minutes.

Serve with your favorite crackers, keeping in mind that thicker crackers work better. I recommend Pepperidge Farm for its wide variety of hearty crackers.

DILL DIP

1 c. sour cream
½ c. mayonnaise
1 Tbsp. dill
¼ onion, finely diced

Mix all ingredients well. Refrigerate for approximately 2 hours.

Serve with bread, crackers, or chips

LAYERED SEAFOOD DIP

- **8 oz. cream cheese**
- **1 c. cottage cheese**
- **¼ c. sour cream**
- **1 Tbsp. horseradish sauce**
- **½ tsp. lemon juice**
- **½ c. cocktail sauce**
- **¼ c. green onion**
- **¼ c. green bell pepper, diced**
- **½ c. black olives, sliced**
- **1 lb. crabmeat or pre-cooked shrimp, peeled and deveined**
- **1 c. shredded cheddar cheese**
- **1 Tbsp. Old Bay seasoning**

Blend cream cheese, Old Bay, cottage cheese, sour cream, horseradish sauce, and lemon juice in food processor until smooth. Add crab or shrimp and mix thoroughly but gently. Spread mixture across the bottom of a large platter or dinner plate. Pour in cocktail sauce; cover with onion, bell pepper, and olives. Top with cheese. Cover and refrigerate 3–4 hours.

Serve with your favorite cracker.

*Recipe can be made with or with out the seafood.

MARIA'S BEER DIP

8 oz. cream cheese, softened

1.1 -oz. package Hidden Valley Dips Mix Fiesta Ranch—dry mix

8 - to 10- oz. shredded taco cheese (three-cheese blend)

6 oz. of beer

Mix together cream cheese, dressing, and shredded cheese. Add beer and mix until smooth. Avoid over-mixing. Dip should be thick. Serve with beer pretzels.

***Drink rest of beer (waste not, want not).

Cheers!

UTZ AND DIP

10 -oz. bag Utz potato chips

8 oz. Philadelphia soft cream cheese

Open container and scoop dip on chip. Hurry—these go fast!

RAVENous-RED PEPPER CHEDDAR DIP

- **10 oz. sharp cheddar cheese**
- **8 oz. cream cheese, softened**
- **½ c. mayonnaise**
- **1 tsp. Tabasco sauce**
- **1 garlic clove, minced**
- **7-oz. jar of roasted red peppers or ½ cup fresh red bell pepper, diced**

Blend cheddar cheese, cream cheese, mayonnaise, Tabasco, and garlic until smooth. Mix in red pepper and stir well.

Ready to serve. This dish can also be made ahead of time and kept in the fridge. If so, let stand for approximately 15–20 minutes at room temperature for the cheeses to soften.

CHEDDAR ONION DIP

- **1 c. Vidalia onion, grated**
- **8 oz. sharp cheddar cheese, grated**
- **8 oz. cream cheese**
- **1 tsp. garlic powder**
- **¼ tsp. cayenne pepper**
- **1–2 drops Tabasco sauce**

Preheat oven to 350°. Mix all ingredients thoroughly. Put in casserole dish and bake until heated through, approximately 20–30 minutes or until bubbly on top. Stir if necessary.

Serve with your favorite cracker.

WHITE BEAN DIP

15.5 -oz. can cannellini beans, drained
1 Tbsp. lemon juice (fresh is best)
1 garlic clove, minced
3 Tbsp. cilantro, finely chopped
1 Tbsp. scallions, diced
3 Tbsp. pistachios or pine nuts, finely chopped (optional)
2 Tbsp. olive oil
Salt and pepper, to taste

Puree beans, lemon juice, garlic, and oil. Mix in scallions, nuts, salt, and pepper. Sprinkle with cilantro.

Serve with toasted pita wedges.

TACO DIP

16 oz. cream cheese, softened
1¼ -oz. package taco seasoning
8 oz. taco sauce
3 plum tomatoes, diced plum tomatoes small
8 oz. shredded cheddar cheese

Mix cream cheese and taco seasoning together. Spread across the bottom of a serving plate (one with a rim). Pour taco sauce over mixture. Top with diced tomatoes and cheese. Serve with tortilla chips.

ARTICHOKE DIP

13 - to 15-oz. can artichoke hearts

¾ c. mayonnaise

½ c. grated Parmesan cheese

⅛ tsp. lemon juice (fresh or bottled)

3 –5 drops Tabasco sauce

Ground black pepper, to taste

Preheat oven to 400°. Chop artichoke hearts into small pieces. Mix all ingredients in a small casserole dish. Bake approximately 15–20 minutes.

*You can play around with this recipe and add more or less mayonnaise or Parmesan to your liking.

GREEN OLIVE TAPENADE

1 c. green olives (without seeds)

¼ c. parsley, chopped

1 c. walnuts, chopped

½ c. green onion, chopped

½ c. vegetable oil

3 Tbsp. lemon juice

½ tsp. crushed red pepper

Combine all ingredients in blender/processor and blend until smooth. Cover and refrigerate for 2–3 hours.

Serve with a firm cracker. Delicious!

*This dish can also be frozen.

STUFFED MUSHROOMS

- **4 large portabella mushrooms,**
- **1 c. asparagus, diced**
- **2 Tbsp. shallots, chopped**
- **2 garlic cloves, minced**
- **1 plum tomato, diced**
- **2 Tbsp. bread crumbs**
- **½ c. grated Parmesan cheese**
- **2 Tbsp. olive oil (I recommend extra virgin)**
- **Salt and pepper, to taste**

Preheat oven to 400°. Remove gills from mushrooms and discard. Wash and remove stems of mushrooms and coarsely chop. Brush 1 tablespoon of olive oil lightly over mushroom caps. Place caps face down (oiled side) on baking sheet. Heat the remaining 1 tablespoon of oil in a medium sized pan on low heat. Add asparagus, shallots, garlic and mushroom stems. Cook until veggies are just starting to get tender. Remove from heat and stir in tomato, salt, and pepper. Spoon mixture into cooked mushroom caps. Combine bread crumbs and cheese and sprinkle on top of caps. Bake at 400° for approximately 10 minutes.

CRAB PRETZEL

- **1 small shallot, diced**
- **8 oz. lump Maryland crabmeat**
- **4 oz. sharp cheddar cheese**
- **3 oz. cream cheese, softened**
- **1½ Tbsp. sour cream**
- **1 Tbsp. mayonnaise**
- **½ tsp. Old Bay seasoning**
- **½ tsp. Worcestershire sauce**
- **½ tsp. Dijon mustard**
- **2 large or 4 medium soft pretzels**

Preheat oven to 375°. Pick crabmeat and mix with, 3 ounces cheddar cheese, cream cheese, sour cream, mayonnaise, Old Bay seasoning, Worcestershire sauce, shallots, and mustard. Refrigerate mixture for approximately 2 hours. Meanwhile, bake pretzel as directed. Spread mixture across the top of each pretzel and top with remaining 1 ounce cheddar cheese. Bake until cheese is melted and completely heated through, approximately 10–13 minutes.

CRAB DIP

- **1 lb. "special" crabmeat, picked**
- **9-oz. bottle French dressing**

Mix crab and dressing well and serve with your favorite cracker.

SHERRY'S SEVEN LAYER DIP

16-oz can refried beans
2 avocados, mashed
2 Tbsp. lemon juice
1¼-oz package taco mix
8 oz. sour cream
½ c. French dressing
¼ c. spring onions, diced
3 medium tomatoes, chopped
Salt and pepper, to taste
8 oz. Monterey Jack cheese
8 oz. cheddar cheese
7-oz. bag tortilla chips

Arrange ingredients on a large serving platter in the following layers:

1. Refried beans
2. Avocados mixed with lemon juice
3. Taco mix—blended with sour cream and French dressing
4. Diced onion
5. Cheddar and Monterey Jack cheeses
6. Tomatoes

When complete, top with additional cheddar cheese and serve with tortilla chips.

BAKED CAPRESE SALAD

1 baguette, sliced into ½ inch pieces (approximately 32 slices)

¼ c. olive oil

5 Roma plum tomatoes, sliced

Ground black pepper, to taste

Sea salt, to taste

1 –2 medium fresh mozzarella balls, thinly sliced

1 c. fresh basil

1 Tbsp. dill

Preheat oven to 450°. Arrange baguettes slices on baking sheet. Brush each piece with oil, then sprinkle with dill and basil. Bake until golden crisp, approximately 5 minutes. Top each baguette slice with tomato, salt, and pepper. Add mozzarella. Put baguette slices and toppings back in oven and bake until cheese is slightly melted and warm, approximately 5 minutes.

BREAKFAST

GOOD Morning!
"jeet yet?"

TOFU SCRAMBLER

1 package extra firm tofu, cubed
½ c. green bell pepper, diced
8 oz. mushrooms, sliced
½ c. Braggs amino acids
¼ c. onion, diced
3 c. water
8 oz. shredded cheddar cheese

Clean mushrooms and sauté in 2 cups water on low heat until tender. When water is reduced to a minimum, add ¼ cup Braggs amino acids. Meanwhile, place tofu in 1 cup water, add onion and green bell pepper. When vegetables are tender and heated through, add mushrooms to mixture. Drain completely. Add remaining ¼ cup of amino acids and stir well. Melt cheese and mix into vegetable mixture.

I like this alone with vegan bacon or on a Thomas's English muffin with butter.

SMOOTHIE

½ c. frozen fruit
½ c. green tea
½ banana
1 scoop protein powder

Put ingredients in a blender and blend until mixed well.

BIRD'S NEST

- **1 loaf French bread, sliced ½ inch thick**
- **2 medium eggs**
- **2 Tbsp. butter**

Melt butter in a skillet over low heat. Meanwhile, scoop a hole in the middle of each slice of bread. Over low to medium heat, place 2 pieces of bread in the skillet and crack an egg in each hole. Keep cooking until desired consistency of the egg is reached.

SCRAMLET

- **6 eggs**
- **3 Tbsp. milk**
- **4 scallions**
- **1 stick butter**
- **8 oz. mushrooms, cleaned and sliced**
- **4 pieces ham, precooked, diced**
- **4 pieces American cheese**

Beat eggs and milk together; add diced ham and scallions. Meanwhile, sauté mushrooms in butter on low heat until tender. Add egg mixture and scramble until eggs are cooked. Top with cheese slices and let melt.

Serve with toast.

BAHAMIAN TOAST

- **1 c. cashews, chopped**
- **1 Tbsp. whole-wheat flour**
- **4 Tbsp. orange juice**
- **1 small banana**
- **1 c. water**
- **6 prunes, chopped**
- **Dash of salt**
- **2 slices of bread**

Preheat oven to 350°. Mix cashews, flour, orange juice, banana, water, prunes, and salt in a blender. Dip both sides of the bread into the mixture and place onto a cookie sheet. Bake until the top is golden brown, approximately 7 minutes. Turn bread to brown on the other side.

Serve with applesauce, fruit or jam.

CREAMED CHIPPED BEEF ON TOAST

- **1 c. milk**
- **2 Tbsp. butter**
- **2 Tbsp. all-purpose flour**
- **2 slices toast**
- **8 oz. chipped beef**

Put butter in saucepan and melt over low heat. Add milk and heat through. Add flour and stir continuously until sauce thickens. Add chipped beef and stir until beef is heated. Pour sauce over toast.

CORNED BEEF HASH

- **2 c. boiled potatoes, diced**
- **1½ c. chopped corned beef**
- **½ small onion, diced**
- **¼ c. heavy cream**
- **3 Tbsp. butter**
- **Salt and pepper, to taste**
- **6 small eggs**

Preheat oven to 450°. Combine potatoes, beef, and onion. Add heavy cream and 1 tablespoon melted butter. Add salt and pepper. Form beef into 6 separate patties and make an indentation on top of each onc. Bake for approximately 15 minutes and remove from oven. Slice remaining 2 tablespoons butter into small squares. Dot the equivalent of 1 tablespoon of butter into each indentation. Crack 1 egg into each indentation, then dot each patty with remaining tablespoon of butter. Bake on 350° until eggs are cooked through, approximately 15–20 minutes.

EGGS À LA GOLDEN POOP

- **2 hard-boiled eggs**
- **2 slices of white toast**
- **Salt and pepper, to taste**
- **1 c. milk**
- **2 Tbsp. butter**
- **2 Tbsp. all-purpose flour**

Put butter in a saucepan and heat through on low heat. Stir in milk. Add flour and stir continuously until sauce thickens. Slice hard-boiled eggs and gently stir into sauce. Season sauce with salt and pepper and pour over toast.

LUNCH

REUBEN

- 2 slices rye bread
- ¼ lb. corned beef
- 2 slices Swiss cheese
- ¼ c. Thousand Island dressing
- 1 c. cooked sauerkraut
- 4 Tbsp. butter

Spread 2 tablespoons butter on one slice of bread and place in frying pan on low heat. Place ½ of the Thousand Island dressing, Swiss cheese, and corned beef on non-buttered side of bread. Top with cooked, hot sauerkraut. Spread remaining 2 tablespoons of butter onto the second piece of bread and place on top of the sauerkraut, butter-side up. Cook until cheese starts to melt, flipping the sandwich halfway through.

DAY-AFTER-THANKSGIVING SANDWICH—LUV DAT SANDWICH

- Leftover turkey
- Leftover stuffing
- Cranberry sauce
- Two slices of bread

Put all ingredients between two pieces of bread and GOBBLE!

THE VONNA-VITCH VEGGIE SUB

- 6 -inch wheat sub roll
- 1½ Tbsp. mayonnaise
- ¼ c. onion, diced
- 5 dill chip pickles
- 6 Green olives, halved
- ¼ green bell pepper
- ½ c. sautéed sliced mushrooms (see note at bottom)
- ½ c. shredded cheddar

Preheat oven to 350°. Place sub roll open faced on baking sheet. Spread mayonnaise on both sides. Top each half of the roll with onion, pickles, olives, bell pepper, and mushrooms. Add cheese. Bake until cheese melts and sub is heated through.

*I sauté my mushrooms in 1 c. water with ¼ c. Worcestershire sauce or Bragg's amino acids for more flavor. I do not recommend using butter or margarine.

SPINACH QUICHE

- 1 refrigerated piecrust, baked as directed
- 10 oz. creamed spinach
- 1 packet Lipton onion soup mix
- 1 c. milk
- 4 small or medium eggs
- 1 c. shredded Swiss cheese

Preheat oven to 350°. Mix spinach, soup mix, milk, eggs, and cheese together thoroughly. Pour mixture into pie shell. Bake for 40–60 minutes.

WRAP IT UP!

- 18 tortillas—different flavors and colors (I recommend red & green for Christmas)
- 16 oz. cream cheese, softened
- 1.1-oz. package Hidden Valley Dips Mix Fiesta Ranch—dry mix
- ½ c. onion, diced
- 4-oz can green chilies, drained
- 4 oz. black olives, chopped
- Few drops of Tabasco sauce

Mix seasoning packet, onion, chilies, olives, and Tabasco sauce together with the cream cheese. Spread the mixture on the tortillas. Roll up each tortilla and slice into 4 pieces. Eat um up yum yum.

CAPRESE PITAS

4 flat pita rounds
1 Tbsp. olive oil
¼ c. grated Parmesan cheese
8-oz. fresh mozzarella ball
3 plum tomatoes, sliced
½ c. packed basil leaves, fresh
¼ c. pine nuts, toasted
1 garlic clove, minced
1 Tbsp. dill

Preheat oven to 450°. Drizzle pita with oil and sprinkle with dill, then Parmesan. Bake approximately 8 minutes. Meanwhile, slice mozzarella and tomatoes and chop toasted pine nuts finely. Combine mozzarella, tomatoes, basil, garlic, and pine nuts. Turn pita over and drizzle with dressing. Cut each round into 6 wedges.

TOMATO SANDWICH

1 medium beefsteak tomato
2 slices wheat bread
3 Tbsp. mayonnaise, to taste
Ground black pepper, to taste
Sea salt, to taste (optional)

Slice tomato. Spread mayonnaise on bread. Add tomato, salt and pepper.

STUFFED TOMATOES

8 medium tomatoes,
2 c. orzo
3 Tbsp. olive oil
⅓ c. fresh basil
1 Tbsp. fresh oregano
1 c. feta cheese, crumbled
2 Tbsp. balsamic vinegar
1 Tbsp. capers
1 tsp. oregano
Salt and pepper (optional)

Preheat oven to 350°. Slice off tops of tomatoes, scoop out and dice the insides of the tomatoes. Meanwhile, cook orzo as directed on package. Mix diced tomatoes, basil, oregano, feta, balsamic vinegar, capers, and oregano with the cooked orzo. Brush the inside of the tomato with olive oil and season with salt and pepper (optional). Cook 10 minutes, drain, stuff with orzo filling. Serve at room temperature.

*I like this recipe using raw tomatoes—cook orzo, mix rest of ingredients and stuff tomatoes.

TUNA ON ENGLISH MUFFIN

6-oz. can tuna
10 green olives, halved
2 Tbsp. mayonnaise
¼ c. onion, diced
½ celery stalk, thinly sliced
2 pieces American cheese
1 Thomas's English Muffin, toasted

Mix tuna, olives, mayonnaise, onion, and celery. Divide mixture between the two muffin halves. Place one piece of cheese on each muffin half. Put in toaster oven or in preheated oven at 350° until cheese melts. Remove from oven and let cool.

TOMATO PIE

4 medium tomatoes, sliced
⅓ c. onion, chopped
1 deep dish piecrust, baked according to package directions
2 Tbsp. fresh basil, diced to small flakes
1 c. shredded cheddar cheese
1 c. shredded mozzarella cheese
½ c. mayonnaise
Salt and pepper, to taste

Preheat oven to 350°. Place tomato, onion, and basil in the baked crust. In a separate dish, mix cheeses and mayonnaise. Spread the cheese mixture evenly over tomatoes, onion and basil. Add salt and pepper. Bake 30 minutes or until cheese is melted.

PITA WITH A PUNCH!

4 whole-wheat pitas
4 plum tomatoes
1 c. baby spinach
1 c. sprouts (any kind)
½ c. plain yogurt
2 Tbsp. tahini
1 garlic clove, minced
1 Tbsp. lemon juice
1 avocado, mashed
1 Tbsp. dill

Mix together yogurt, tahini, garlic, and lemon juice. Add tomatoes and spinach; mix well. Stuff each pita with mixture. Add avocado, then sprouts, and sprinkle with dill.

PEPPERONI ROLLS

1 loaf frozen unbaked bread dough, thawed
8-oz. stick pepperoni, thinly sliced
12 oz. Velveeta cheese, sliced

Slice bread into ½- to 1-inch slices and flatten with fingers. Add a few pepperoni slices and then add chunks of cheese. Fold bread and pinch edges together. Cook on greased cookie sheet as directed on bread package.

*This goes great with your favorite tomato soup.

ITALIAN COLD CUT

2 Tbsp. sesame oil
Sliced ham
1 –2 slices of white onion
Swiss cheese
Sliced salami
Provolone
Lettuce
Tomato
2 Tbsp. mayonnaise
1 Tbsp. Sesame oil
6 -inch sub roll

Drizzle sesame oil on bottom half of roll and spread mayonnaise on top half of roll. Add meat, onion, cheese, lettuce, and tomato.

CUCUMBER SANDWICH

2 slices white bread
½ cucumber sliced
3 Tbsp. mayonnaise
1 Tbsp. dill

Mix dill and mayonnaise (add more dill to taste, if necessary). Spread mixture onto each piece of bread. Add cucumber slices.

SHRIMP SALAD

1 b. steamed shrimp, peeled, deveined and cut into bite-sized pieces

½ c. mayonnaise

½ c. onion, diced

2 Tbsp. Old Bay seasoning

¼ c. celery, very thinly sliced

⅛ Tabasco sauce (optional)

Ground black pepper, to taste

Place cut shrimp in a bowl. Add mayonnaise, onion, celery, Old Bay, Tabasco, and pepper and mix well.

Enjoy this as a sandwich on your favorite bread or roll, or place one cup rounded mound on a bed of lettuce to enjoy as a salad. You can also enjoy this dish as a dip by scooping it onto your favorite cracker.

Scrumptious!

EGG MELT SANDWICH

- 1 small or medium egg
- 2 slices white bread
- ½ -inch slice Velveeta cheese, cut into chunks
- 2 Tbsp. mayonnaise
- 2 slices tomato
- Salt and pepper, to taste

Fry egg in pan over low heat. After a few seconds, flip the egg and break the yolk. Cook a few seconds more so that the egg is cooked but the yolk is not cooked through. Meanwhile, toast bread. Spread mayonnaise on both slices of toast and add tomato, salt, pepper, and cheese. Place hot egg on top of cheese and allow the cheese to melt.

MEATLOAF SANDWICH

- 1 thick slice leftover meatloaf
- 2 slices of white bread
- ¼ c. ketchup
- Salt and pepper, to taste

Spread ketchup on each piece of bread. Microwave meatloaf and place on bread. Add salt and pepper to taste.

MARYLAND CRAB CAKE SANDWICHES

- **1 lb. Maryland lump crabmeat**
- **½ c. mayonnaise**
- **1 celery stalk, finely diced**
- **1 tsp. wet yellow mustard**
- **⅛ tsp. Worcestershire sauce**
- **1 tsp. Old Bay seasoning**
- **½ c. onion, diced**
- **1 tsp. parsley**
- **1 small egg**
- **Pepper, to taste**
- **¼ c. Italian bread crumbs**
- **1 sandwich roll**
- **Dash of Tabasco sauce**

Pick through meat to remove bones. Mix together crabmeat, mayonnaise, celery, mustard, Worcestershire, Tabasco, Old Bay seasoning, onion, parsley, egg, and pepper. Form mixture into cakes and broil until golden on both sides. Serve on a roll with your favorite toppings. Tartar sauce and mustard also go well with this sandwich.

COTTAGE CHEESE PIE

1 pre-made refrigerated 9-inch pie shell
1 lb. potatoes
1 c. cottage cheese
½ c. sour cream
2 Tbsp. chives
1 Tbsp. mayonnaise
½ stick butter
1 tsp. dill (optional)
Salt and pepper, to taste

Preheat oven to 450°. Grease pie dish and lay out the pie shell. Bake 10 minutes. Meanwhile, boil potatoes until tender, drain and mash. Add cottage cheese, mayo, dill, chives, salt, pepper, and sour cream and mash until blended. Pour mixture into pie shell and spread evenly. Top with pats of butter. Reduce heat to 350° and cook 20–25 minutes.

BLACK DOG (No Led Zepplin here)

1 package hot dogs (your choice)
Hot dog rolls
Your favorite toppings

Place an individual hot dog on a fork, hold over the flame of a stove and rotate until the entire dog is black. Serve on roll with your favorite condiment or cut and eat alone (with ketchup is best).

BROCCOLI-AND-HAM PASTA SALAD

- ½ c. mayonnaise
- ⅓ c. plain yogurt
- ½ c. sour cream
- 3 Tbsp. rice vinegar
- 1 Tbsp. Dijon mustard
- 1 Tbsp. honey
- ¼ c. yellow onion, diced
- 1¼ tsp. dill
- White pepper, to taste
- Celery salt, to taste
- 3 c. small sea shell pasta
- 4 c. broccoli florets, chopped
- 8 oz. ham, diced
- ¼ c. red onion, diced
- ¼ c. red bell pepper, diced
- ¼ c. green bell pepper, diced
- ¼ c. yellow bell pepper, diced
- ½ c. raisins
- 4 c. baby spinach leaves
- 1 c. mixed lettuce

Cook pasta according to package directions. Boil broccoli until tender, drain. Meanwhile, prepare the dressing: mix mayonnaise, yogurt, sour cream, vinegar, mustard, honey, yellow onions, dill, salt and pepper in a bowl and mix well. Adjust seasonings to taste. In a separate bowl, combine pasta, broccoli, ham, peppers, red onions and raisins. Pour dressing mix over pasta and mix well. Chill for thirty minutes. Serve on a bed of spinach and lettuce.

DINNERS

LINGUINI WITH CLAM SAUCE

4 garlic cloves, crushed
½ c. olive oil
1 Tbsp. all-purpose flour
4 6½-oz. cans chopped clams (do not drain)
1½ c. fresh parsley
16-oz. package linguine
½ c. cooking sherry
Salt and pepper, to taste

Sauté garlic in olive oil on low heat until golden. Gradually stir in flour, clams, parsley and sherry. Stir constantly until sauce thickens. Meanwhile, cook linguine as directed on package. Serve sauce over linguine.

DIANE'S BUM STEW

1 lb. ground beef
15¼-oz. can whole kernel corn
10¾-oz can Campbell's tomato soup
½ onion, diced
7¼-oz. package Kraft Macaroni and Cheese
2 pieces American cheese

Preheat oven to 350°. Prepare macaroni according to package directions. Brown ground beef over low to medium heat and drain. Mix in the corn, soup, onion, and macaroni. Top with sliced pieces of American cheese. Bake until heated through and cheese is melted on top, approximately 30 minutes.

HURRY CURRY

- **3 3-oz. packages chicken-flavored ramen noodles**
- **¼ c. chopped onion**
- **1 tsp. curry powder**
- **½ c. milk**
- **2 Tbsp. butter**
- **10¾-oz. can cream of chicken soup**
- **1 Tbsp. lemon juice**
- **6 oz. chicken, precooked, cut into chunks**
- **½ c. mayonnaise**

Preheat oven to 350°. Cook noodles according to package directions. Drain; mix with seasoning and set aside. Melt butter in pan, add onion and cook over low heat until golden. Add mayonnaise, milk, soup, and lemon juice and mix thoroughly. Cook until heated through. Do not boil. Mix in noodles, curry, and precooked chicken. Bake for approximately 30 minutes.

*I also use this as a side dish and omit the chicken. To make it meatless, you can use cream of celery soup and omit chicken.

CHICKEN LINGUINE

28-oz. can crushed tomatoes, liquid drained
1 beef bouillon cube, crushed to powder
2 Tbsp. Italian seasoning
2 tsp. garlic powder
1 tsp. pepper
Pinch of salt
1 c. green bell pepper, diced
1 c. red bell pepper, diced
8 oz. mushrooms, sliced
½ cup onion, diced
1 Tbsp. parsley
1 Tbsp. walnut oil
16-oz. package linguini noodles
3 medium-sized chicken breasts,
1 tsp. Cajon seasoning

Preheat oven to 350°. Bake chicken until cooked through. When chicken is no longer pink in the center, remove from oven and cut into chunks. Cook linguine according to package directions and drain; set aside. Mix walnut oil, pepper, mushrooms, onion, parsley, bouillon powder, Italian seasoning, garlic powder, pepper, salt, Cajon seasoning, tomatoes, and chicken in a saucepan. Cook on low heat until blended, approximately 15 minutes. Pour over linguini and mix well.

SMIDGE OF MIDGE

1 lb. ground beef
¼ c. onion, chopped
½ c. barbeque sauce
3 pieces American cheese
2 8-oz. cans Pillsbury crescent rolls (don't pull dough apart)

Brown ground beef with onion on low heat; drain well. Stir in barbeque sauce. Meanwhile, unroll 1 can of dough on an ungreased cookie sheet. Pinch all perforations together, creating one large rectangle of dough. Form beef mixture into a loaf and place on top of unrolled dough, leaving a ½ inch border to fold. Top the loaf with cheese. Unroll second can of dough and pinch all perforations together, creating another large rectangle of dough. Place second piece of dough over top of loaf and pinch edges together with the edges of the bottom piece of dough Bake as directed on dough package.

MAMA WHAT A PASTA!

¼ c. olive oil
4 garlic cloves, minced
1 c. shiitake mushrooms (I recommend frozen)
12-oz. package penne pasta
8 oz. mozzarella
16 oz. fresh baby spinach
Salt and pepper, to taste

Cook pasta according to package directions. Meanwhile, sauté garlic and mushrooms in oil on low heat for 2 minutes. Add spinach and cook until wilted, approximately 5 minutes. Stir in cheese. Mix with pasta. Season with salt and pepper.

QUICK PASTA

16-oz. penne pasta
3 Tbsp. olive oil
2 garlic cloves, minced
5 large tomatoes, sliced into ½-inch chunks
2 Tbsp. balsamic vinegar
1 tsp. Worcestershire sauce
¼ c. pine nuts
2 Tbsp. fresh basil
2 Tbsp. grated Parmesan cheese
Sea salt and ground pepper

Cook pasta as directed. In a separate pan, heat oil on low heat. Add garlic and pine nuts and sauté for approximately 1–2 minutes. Add tomatoes, vinegar, Worcestershire, salt, and pepper and cook until tomatoes are tender, approximately 10 minutes. Stir in basil. Add sauce to cooked pasta and sprinkle with Parmesan.

BEEF BURGUNDY—Mouth Watering!

2 lbs. beef stew meat, cut into chunks
10¾-oz can cream of mushroom soup
2-oz. package Lipton Onion Soup and Dip Mix 2 oz
8- to 10- oz. fresh mushrooms, sliced
½ c. burgundy wine

Preheat oven to 325°. Thoroughly mix all ingredients together. Cover and bake in casserole dish 2½ hours, stirring once or twice. Add a little bit of water if mixture becomes too dry.

BAKED SHRIMP

1 large garlic clove, minced
¾ c. butter, softened
1 tsp. salt
⅛ tsp. marjoram
1 c. fine bread crumbs
½ c. cooking sherry
3 lbs. shrimp, peeled and deveined
1 small lemon, sliced into wedges
3 Tbsp. parsley, finely chopped
A dash of Tabasco
⅛ tsp. tarragon

Preheat oven to 400°. Combine garlic, butter, salt, tarragon, marjoram and Tabasco and cream together. Add bread crumbs and sherry. Toss until well blended. Add shrimp and toss until shrimp are lightly coated with bread crumb mixture. Divide shrimp and sprinkle each with chopped parsley. Bake for 20–25 minutes. Lightly squeeze lemon wedges over shrimp before serving.

PASTA PRIMAVERA

12 oz. pasta (your choice, though I recommend angel hair)
3 green onions, diced
4 Tbsp. olive oil
2 garlic cloves, minced
½ c. asparagus, trimmed and cut into pieces
1 c. heavy whipping cream
½ c. red bell pepper, cut into small pieces
½ c. yellow bell pepper, cut into small pieces
½ c. green bell pepper, cut into small pieces
½ tsp. crushed red pepper
½ c. grated Parmesan cheese
¼ c. fresh basil, diced
Salt and pepper, to taste (optional)

Cook pasta according to package directions. Add basil and Parmesan and toss with noodles. Meanwhile, slice green onion and sauté in oil until golden. Add garlic, asparagus, and bell peppers. Cook 6–7 minutes until veggies are tender but not mushy. Stir in cream and crushed red pepper. If desired, add salt and pepper to taste. Heat mixture until boiling.

BAKED FISH

½ cup water
1½ stick butter
Lemon pepper, to taste
4 medium filets of flounder

Preheat oven to 350°. Pour water in bottom of pan, add fish, and cover with lemon pepper. Cut butter into pieces and add to pan. Bake uncovered for 15 minutes. Flip fish over and add ½ stick of butter and more water if necessary. Sprinkle fish with more lemon pepper and cook 15 minutes more or until fish flakes.

BARBEQUE SAUCE PORK CHOPS

4 medium pork chops
½ c. salad oil
½ c. lemon juice
½ c. wine vinegar
¼ c. soy sauce
Salt and pepper, to taste
1 tsp. oregano

Preheat oven to 350°. Combine salad oil, lemon juice, wine vinegar and soy sauce. Add salt, fresh ground pepper, and oregano. Cover and refrigerate overnight. Pour sauce evenly over pork chops. Cook for 30 minutes or until cooked through.

BUTTER LASAGNA

- 8 oz. lasagna noodles
- 2 10-oz. packages frozen spinach, precooked, drained
- 2 lbs. cottage cheese
- 1 Tbsp. fresh parsley, chopped
- ¾ c. butter, softened (do not use margarine)
- 1 lb. shredded Monterey or mozzarella cheese
- ¾ c. grated Parmesan cheese
- 2 garlic cloves, pressed
- Salt and pepper, to taste

Preheat oven to 350°. Cook lasagna noodles according to package directions. Meanwhile, mix cottage cheese, parsley, ½ cup butter, salt and pepper, spinach and garlic in bowl. Place a layer of cooked lasagna noodles in a pan; follow with one layer each of cottage cheese mixture, shredded cheese, spinach, and Parmesan. Repeat layering until all ingredients have been used up, finishing with a layer of shredded cheese. Dot the dish with remaining ¼ cup butter. Bake for 30 minutes.

ITALIAN ZITI

½ lb. mild Italian sausage, thinly sliced
1 stick butter
8 oz. mushrooms, sliced
1 c. green bell pepper, diced
½ c. onion, diced
⅓ c. all-purpose flour
2½ c. milk
2 c. shredded cheddar cheese
½ c. grated Parmesan cheese
½ tsp. ground black pepper
8 oz. ziti

Preheat oven to 350°. Cook pasta according to package directions. Brown sausage and drain fat; set aside. Melt 1 stick of butter and cook mushrooms, green bell pepper, and onion on low heat until tender but not browned. Blend in flour and gradually stir in milk. Cook over medium heat, stirring constantly, until mixture begins to boil. Blend in 1½ cups cheddar cheese, Parmesan cheese, and pepper until cheeses are melted and mixture is smooth. Add cooked pasta and sausage. Mix well. Pour mixture into a casserole dish and dot with remaining stick of butter. Top with remaining ½ cup cheddar cheese. Bake covered for 30 minutes or until heated through.

TUNA NOODLE CASSEROLE

6-oz. can tuna
15-oz. can cream of celery soup
12-oz. package egg noodles
1 c. milk
Croutons (optional)

Preheat oven to 350°. Cook noodles according to package directions. Meanwhile, mix soup and milk. Add tuna. Combine mixture with noodles and mix well. Add more milk if dish is too dry. Bake until heated through, approximately 30 minutes. Top with croutons if desired.

CODDIE CAKES

2 small to medium pieces of codfish, soaked over night
½ c. mayonnaise
½ c. bread crumbs
1 egg
2 Tbsp. parsley
1 tsp. lemon juice
¼ c. vegetable oil

Heat oil on medium heat. Meanwhile, rinse codfish dry, flake, and check for bones. Mix codfish together with mayonnaise, bread crumbs, egg, parsley, and lemon juice. Shape cod mixture into patties and fry in hot oil, flattening cakes in the pan. Fry on medium heat until golden, approximately 5 minutes on each side.

Serve with yellow mustard and crackers.

CHICKEN FRICASSEE—Pass the Shicken…

2 Tbsp. butter

1 small onion, diced

1 garlic clove, minced

½ c. chicken broth

½ c. whipping cream

1 c. chicken, precooked, cut into chunks

1 tsp. thyme

1 tsp. tarragon

½ tsp. dill

12-oz. package egg noodles

10 oz. mushrooms, sliced

Salt and pepper, to taste

Cook noodles according to package directions. Meanwhile, melt butter in skillet on low heat; add onion and cook until golden. Add garlic and chicken and cook for a few minutes more, stirring often. Add mushrooms and chicken broth and cook for approximately 3 minutes, stirring often. Stir in cream, thyme, tarragon, dill, salt, and pepper. Cook over low heat until sauce begins to thicken. Serve over cooked noodles.

BROCCOLI-CHICKEN—
"Salsa Laurie says it's the BEST!"

2 small chicken breasts, precooked, diced
3 garlic cloves, minced
16-oz. package rigatoni
¾ c. chicken bouillon
¼ tsp. crushed red pepper
1 small head of broccoli, coarsely chopped
1 Tbsp. olive oil
4 Tbsp. grated Parmesan cheese
1 Tbsp. lemon juice
Salt and pepper, to taste

Cook pasta according to package directions. Meanwhile, in 1 tablespoon olive oil, cook garlic in a saucepan on low heat. Add broth, red pepper, and broccoli; cover and cook 5 minutes. Uncover and add lemon juice, salt, pepper, and Parmesan and cook until heated through. Toss with pasta. Add chicken, and gently toss again. Let stand 5 minutes before serving.

SALISBURY STEAK

- 2 lbs. ground beef
- ½ c. bread crumbs
- 1 small onion, finely chopped
- 1 egg, beaten
- ¾ c. milk
- 8 oz. fresh mushrooms, sliced
- 12-oz. package egg noodles
- 26-oz can condensed cream of mushroom soup
- 1 tsp. Worcestershire sauce
- Pepper, to taste

Preheat oven to 425°. Prepare egg noodles according to package directions. Mix ½ cup soup, Worcestershire, beef, bread crumbs, onion and egg. Shape mixture into 8 firm patties, each approximately ½ inch thick. Bake for approximately 15 minutes. Meanwhile, in a medium bowl, combine the remaining soup, milk, sliced mushrooms and pepper. Spoon mushroom mixture over patties. Bake an additional 10 minutes or until completely cooked through. Serve over egg noodles.

CRAB IMPERIAL

- **1 c. dry sherry**
- **1 Tbsp. shallots, finely chopped**
- **1 small green bell pepper, finely chopped**
- **3 - to 4- oz. jar pimentos, chopped**
- **½ c. heavy cream**
- **1 egg**
- **1 tsp. dry mustard**
- **1 lb. lump Maryland crabmeat, picked**
- **1 c. mayonnaise**

Bring sherry to a boil; stir in shallots, green bell pepper, and pimentos. Cook over medium heat, stirring occasionally, until only a small amount of liquid remains. In a separate dish, mix together heavy cream and egg, then stir into shallot mixture. Add dry mustard. Remove from heat and gently stir in crabmeat. Let cool; add mayonnaise. Place evenly into individual baking dishes or serve in a one-quart dish.

WEEKLY'S SUKIYAKI

1 lb. stew beef
1 small bag of carrots, thinly sliced
1 celery stalk, diced
1 small onion, chopped coarsely
5 small potatoes, cut into chunks
2 c. beef stock
¼ c. ketchup
1 bay leaf
12-oz. can cut green beans
1 Tbsp. olive oil
3 Tbsp. all-purpose flour
1 Tbsp. cornstarch

Roll meat in flour. Heat olive oil in pan on low heat; add meat and brown until cooked through. Add onion and cook until golden. Mix in carrots, celery, potatoes, ketchup, bay leaf, green beans, and 1 cup beef stock. Simmer on low heat for 2–3 hours or until vegetables and meat are tender. During the last half hour, in a separate dish, mix together cornstarch and remaining 1 cup beef stock. Add mixture to stew and stir until the stew is thick. (add water if necessary)

JIMMY'S GAWUMPKI

1 c. white rice
1 small head of cabbage
1 lb. ground beef
Salt and pepper, to taste
1 c. onion, diced
¼ c. ketchup
2 c. water

Preheat oven to 400°. Cook rice according to package directions. Meanwhile, brown ground beef in skillet. Core cabbage and cook in a covered pan with water for about 5 minutes to soften. Drain and peel apart leaves. In a separate dish, mix beef with ketchup, rice, ½ cup onion, salt, and pepper. Place a scoop of beef mixture into a small leaf, then wrap with larger leaf and place in an oblong pan. Continue to do this until all cabbage and beef mixture are used up. Top leaves with remaining ½ cup onion and drizzle with a little extra water. Bake for approximately 1½ hours.

MOM'S SALMON CAKES

16 oz. canned salmon, drained
½ c. mayonnaise
½ c. bread crumbs
1 Tbsp. parsley
¼ c. onion, diced
1 egg
Pepper, to taste
Vegetable oil (optional)

Mix together salmon, mayonnaise, bread crumbs, parsley, onion, egg, and pepper. Shape the mixture into patties and broil or fry in vegetable oil until browned on both sides. Serve on a roll or with crackers.

SIDES

ASPARAGUS BUNDLES

8 oz. asparagus, trimmed

1 medium red bell pepper, sliced

1 medium yellow bell pepper, sliced

1 medium green bell pepper, sliced

1 Tbsp. butter

2 oz. cream cheese, softened

1 Tbsp. pesto (homemade or from store)

11-oz. can breadstick dough

Preheat oven to 375°. Add asparagus and peppers to boiling water and boil until tender (but not mushy). Drain and add butter. In a separate dish, mix together pesto and cream cheese. Separate the dough into individual breadsticks and spread the pesto/cream cheese mixture on each. Top each stick with peppers. Wrap dough around peppers in a crisscross fashion and place on baking sheet seam-side down. Bake 15 minutes or until dough is cooked through.

SAUERKRAUT

2 16-oz. cans sauerkraut

1 lb. kielbasa, thinly sliced

1 tsp. caraway seeds

28 oz. water (use sauerkraut cans)

Cook on low heat for 3–4 hours or until kielbasa is cooked through. Stir occasionally and add more water as necessary.

CHICKEN BROCCOLI STUFFING

26-oz. can cream of mushroom condensed soup
2 c. milk
12-oz. package Pepperidge Farm Herb Seasoned Cube Stuffing
3 c. chicken breast, precooked, cut into chunks
2 10-oz. packages frozen broccoli, chopped, thawed, and drained
1 c. celery, chopped
8 oz. shredded Swiss cheese

Preheat oven to 375°. Combine soup and milk until blended. Stir in stuffing, chicken, broccoli and celery. Bake for 35 minutes. Remove dish from oven and sprinkle with cheese. Put dish back in oven and heat 5 more minutes or until cheese is melted.

BBQ LENTILS

1 Tbsp. olive oil
½ c. red onion, chopped
1 tsp. garlic, minced
2 tsp. chili powder
1 tsp. dry mustard
2 c. beef bouillon
1 c. tomato sauce
3 Tbsp. balsamic vinegar
1 Tbsp. Dijon mustard
2 Tbsp. honey
1½ c. brown lentils, rinsed
Pepper, to taste

Heat oil, add onion and cook on low heat until softened. Add garlic, chili powder, dry mustard, and pepper. Cook approximately one minute. Add bouillon, tomato sauce, vinegar, Dijon mustard, honey, and lentils. Mix well. Cover and simmer 30 minutes or until lentils are tender but not mushy. Add water a little at a time if needed.

VONNIE'S POETATO SALAD

- 3 large baking potatoes
- ¾ c. mayonnaise
- 1 tsp. wet yellow mustard
- 1 tsp. cider vinegar
- ½ c. onion, diced
- 1½ celery stalks, very thinly sliced
- 2 Tbsp. celery seed

Cut potatoes into chunks (with skin) and boil until soft enough for a fork to pass through, approximately 5–10 minutes (do not overcook). Strain and let cool. Peel skin and cut into bite size pieces. Add mayonnaise, vinegar, and mustard and mix well. Add onion, celery, and celery seed and chill for at least 2–3 hours. Before serving, mix again and adjust ingredients to taste.

ZUCCHINI AND EGGPLANT CASSEROLE

3 medium zucchini, thinly sliced
2 large red bell peppers, diced
1 small onion, diced
1 small eggplant, chopped
2 cloves garlic, minced
2 Tbsp. olive oil
½ c. mayonnaise
½ c. grated Parmesan cheese
2 c. shredded mozzarella cheese
1 package Ritz crackers, crushed
Salt and pepper, to taste

Preheat oven to 350°. Heat olive oil in a large skillet on low heat. Add zucchini, red bell pepper, onion, eggplant, garlic, salt, and pepper. Sauté until vegetables are soft but not mushy; stir often. In a separate bowl, combine mayonnaise, Parmesan cheese, and 1 cup mozzarella cheese. Add vegetable mixture and mix well. Cover the bottom of a casserole dish with half of the package of crushed Ritz crackers. Evenly spread vegetable and cheese mixture over crackers. Top with remaining ½ package of crackers and remaining cup of mozzarella cheese. Bake uncovered for 20–25 minutes. Let stand 5–10 minutes before serving.

STUFFING

2 tsp. vegetable oil
1 medium onion, chopped
3 celery ribs, chopped
1 Tbsp. sage
2 garlic cloves, minced
1½ c. milk
½ c. chicken broth
12 - to 16- oz. package whole wheat bread crumbs
½ lb. sausage (of your choice), fully cooked and chopped
Salt and pepper, to taste

Heat oven to 350° and lightly grease casserole dish. In a separate pan, sauté onion, celery and garlic in oil on low heat until the onion is golden. Add sage, milk, broth, and sausage and stir well. Remove from heat; add bread crumbs, salt, and pepper. Place mixture in the casserole dish; cover with foil and bake for 30 minutes. If the stuffing is too dry, add more broth. Remove foil and continue to bake until top is crisp and brown, approximately 10 minutes longer.

GREEK PEPPERS WITH QUINOA

- **4 bell peppers, any combination of red, green, yellow or orange, chopped**
- **15-oz. can chickpeas**
- **1 Tbsp. olive oil**
- **8 oz. baby spinach**
- **1½ c. quinoa**
- **¾ c. feta cheese, crumbled**
- **¼ c. sundried tomatoes, coarsely chopped**
- **2 Tbsp. red wine vinegar**
- **1 tsp. capers**
- **¼ c. onion, diced**

Cook quinoa according to package directions. Meanwhile, sauté onion and bell peppers in oil on low heat until onion are golden. Add spinach and stir frequently until spinach starts to wilt. Add chickpeas, tomatoes, vinegar, and capers. Mix well. Add cooked vegetables to quinoa and mix. Top with feta.

ORZO SALAD

16-oz. box orzo

1 Tbsp. olive oil

2 garlic cloves, minced

10-oz. package fresh baby spinach

6-oz. can black olives

8 oz. feta cheese, crumbled

4-oz. jar sun dried tomatoes in oil cut into strips (do not drain)

2 Tbsp. pine nuts

Cook orzo according to package directions. Add 2 tablespoons of oil from the jar of sundried tomatoes; mix well. Meanwhile, heat oil in a saucepan. Add garlic and cook for a few seconds. Add pine nuts and cook a few seconds more. Add spinach and cook until it just starts to wilt. Place garlic and spinach in a bowl and add olives, tomatoes, and feta and mix well. Add mixture to orzo and mix well.

TORTELLINI YVONNE

8 -to 12- oz. box tri-color cheese tortellini
1 pepperoni stick, cut into chunks
1 medium or large tomato, diced
½ c. onion, diced
8 oz. sharp cheese, diced
¾ c. green olives, diced
½ c. mayonnaise
1 Tbsp. dill
⅛ t celery salt
⅛ tsp. oregano
1 tsp. basil
⅛ tsp. garlic salt
Pepper, to taste

Cook tortellini according to package directions, drain and place in a serving bowl. Add mayonnaise while tortellini is still warm and mix. Add dill, celery salt, oregano, basil, pepper, and garlic salt and mix well. Stir in pepperoni, tomatoes, onion, cheese, and olives, and adjust to taste if necessary. Add mixture to tortellini and serve.

TORTELLINI SALAD II

8 - to 12- oz. package tortellini (any kind of filling)

⅓ c. olive oil

3 Tbsp. red wine vinegar

2 garlic cloves, crushed

1 Tbsp. basil

⅛ tsp. crushed red pepper

Salt, to taste

1 small head of broccoli, cut into bite size pieces

1 c. cherry tomatoes, halved

½ c. pepperoni, cut into chunks

¼ c. grated Parmesan cheese

Cook tortellini according to package directions. Drain well, put in serving bowl and add oil, vinegar, garlic, basil, crushed red pepper, and salt and mix well. Add Parmesan while pasta is still warm and toss to coat. Refrigerate 2–3 hours. Add broccoli, tomatoes, and pepperoni. Mix well and serve.

VEGETABLE GRATIN

3 medium zucchini, diced
1 medium yellow squash, diced
14-oz. can artichoke hearts, drained, diced
¼ c. bread crumbs (recommend Italian)
¼ c. onion, diced
1½ c. shredded Swiss cheese
½ c. half and half
4 Tbsp. grated Parmesan cheese
1 tsp. oregano
½ Tbsp. flour
Dash of salt and pepper

Heat oven to 350°. In large bowl mix zucchini, squash, artichokes, bread crumbs, oregano, flour, salt, pepper and onion. Spread half of squash mixture over the bottom of a lightly greased baking dish. In a separate dish, mix half and half, Swiss cheese, and Parmesan cheese and spread over squash mixture. Repeat layering with squash and cheese mixtures. Drizzle with half and half. Bake 50 minutes or until squash is tender.

BROCCOLI CASSEROLE

- **4 10-oz. packages frozen broccoli, chopped**
- **2 packages Ritz crackers, crushed**
- **½ c. chopped onion**
- **1 stick butter**
- **12 oz. Velveeta cheese**
- **2 Tbsp. milk**

Preheat oven to 350°. Spread one package of crushed Ritz crackers in the bottom of a casserole dish. Cook and drain broccoli and onion and layer on top of crackers. In a separate dish, cut Velveeta into chunks and melt. Add milk and stir. Pour milk and cheese mixture over broccoli and onion. Sprinkle second package of crackers over broccoli. Melt butter and pour over crackers. Bake until heated through, approximately 20 minutes.

ZUCCHINI CASSEROLE

- **3 medium zucchini, diced**
- **1 large red bell pepper, diced**
- **½ c. onion, diced**
- **1 small eggplant, diced**
- **2 garlic cloves, minced**
- **3 Tbsp. olive oil**
- **½ c. mayonnaise**
- **½ c. grated Parmesan cheese**
- **8 oz. shredded mozzarella cheese**
- **8 Ritz crackers, crushed**

Preheat oven to 350°. Sauté zucchini, eggplant, pepper, onion and garlic in oil on low heat until tender, approximately 10–13 minutes. Meanwhile, mix mayonnaise, Parmesan and 1 cup mozzarella. Combine cheese mixture with veggie mixture and spread evenly in a casserole dish. Top with remaining mozzarella and cracker crumbs. Bake uncovered 20–25 minutes. Let stand 10 minutes before serving.

SOUPS

Tried and True

RED PEPPER AND CRAB BISQUE

- 2 Tbsp. butter
- ½ c. yellow onion, finely chopped
- ½ c. celery, thinly sliced
- 1½ c. red bell pepper, diced
- 2 tsp. Old Bay seasoning
- 3 c. chicken bouillon
- 3 c. water
- ½ medium potato, diced
- ½ c. half and half
- 1 lb. crabmeat (lump is best)
- Salt and pepper, to taste

Melt butter in a pan. Add onion, celery, red bell pepper and Old Bay. Cover and cook on low heat, stirring occasionally, approximately 10 minutes. Add bouillon, water, and potatoes and bring to a boil. Reduce heat; cover partially and simmer until potatoes are tender, approximately 30 minutes. Divide the mixture into batches and puree each batch in a blender. Return the batches to saucepan. Add half and half and bring to a simmer on low heat. Mix in crabmeat, salt, and pepper. Cook until heated through, approximately 5 minutes.

*For a vegetarian option, omit crabmeat and use chicken bouillon.

ZUCCHINI SOUP

- ½ c. onion, diced
- 2 bacon slices, precooked, crumbled
- 1 small zucchini, peeled,
- 2 chicken bouillon cubes
- 2 cups water
- ½ c. brown rice
- 2 Tbsp. butter

Sauté onion and bacon in butter until bacon is soft. Meanwhile, slice zucchini into coin-sized pieces. Cut each coin-sized piece in half. Add zucchini slices to onion and bacon and let simmer. While the vegetables and bacon are cooking, bring bouillon cubes and water to a boil in a separate pot. Add rice; cover and simmer for approximately 10 minutes or until rice is done. Mix in onion, bacon and zucchini.

BROCCOLI SOUP

- 4 c. chicken broth
- 10 oz. broccoli, chopped
- 1 c. milk
- 1 small onion, diced
- 3 Tbsp. butter
- 2 Tbsp. all-purpose flour

Sauté broccoli and onion in 2 tablespoons butter on low heat until tender. In a blender, mix vegetables with 2 cups broth and puree. Heat milk and remaining 2 cups of broth over low heat for 5 minutes. Add flour and remaining 1 tablespoon of butter, stirring constantly until broth comes to a boil. Add vegetable puree to the broth mixture and simmer 10 minutes.

MUSHROOM BISQUE

4 c. mushrooms, sliced
1 small onion, diced
2 c. vegetable bouillon
6 Tbsp. butter
6 Tbsp. all-purpose flour
2 c. milk
1 c. heavy cream
Salt and pepper, to taste
½ c. cooking sherry

In a pot, add mushrooms and onion to bouillon. Cover and simmer on low heat 30 minutes. In a separate pan, melt butter and slowly whisk in flour until smooth mixture is formed. Add milk and bring mixture to a boil, stirring constantly. Combine stock mixture and cream; stir well. Add sherry and cook until heated through, approximately 5 minutes. Season with salt and pepper.

I like this soup best after it sits for a day in the refrigerator.

CREAM OF CARROT SOUP

1½ c. carrots, sliced
1 small onion, chopped
2 Tbsp. butter
2½ c. chicken bouillon or vegetable stock
¼ c. brown rice
1 c. heavy cream
2 celery stalks, finely chopped

Melt butter in pan. Sauté carrots, celery, and onion over low heat for approximately 10 minutes, stirring constantly. Add stock or bouillon, and bring to a gentle boil. Add rice. Cover pot and simmer at least 20 minutes or until tender. Allow to cool. Pour soup and ½ cup cream into a blender and puree until smooth (this may need to be done in batches). Stir in the rest of the heavy cream and serve.

This soup can be served both hot and cold.

PASTA FAGIOLI

- 1 Tbsp. olive oil
- ½ c. onion, chopped
- 2 garlic cloves, minced
- ¼ tsp. crushed red pepper
- 19-oz. can cannellini beans, drained
- 4 c. chicken broth
- 15-oz. can diced tomatoes
- ½ c. ditalini pasta
- ¼ c. grated Parmesan cheese

Sauté onion and garlic in olive oil on low heat until golden. Add red pepper, beans, crushed red pepper, and broth and bring to a boil. Reduce heat and add tomatoes and pasta. Simmer 10 minutes or until pasta is tender. Sprinkle with Parmesan. Mangia!

ASPARAGUS SOUP

¼ c. butter
1 c. onion, diced
½ c. white wine
1 tsp. lemon juice
½ c. all-purpose flour
4 c. chicken bouillon
2 c. milk
½ c. heavy cream
1 bundle of asparagus, trimmed and chopped
Salt and pepper, to taste

Sauté onion and asparagus in butter and lemon juice on low heat until softened (but not mushy). Add wine, bring to a boil and cook 1–2 minutes. Whisk flour into bouillon and bring to boil, stirring until thick. Reduce heat and stir in milk. Simmer 5 minutes. Puree mixture in a blender (mixture may have to be divided into batches) and return to pot. Stir in cream. Cook until heated through. Season with salt and pepper.

VICHYSSOISE—Pastor Joe says, "Mmmm good, good, good good"

3 medium leek bulbs, thinly sliced
½ c. onion, chopped
3 Tbsp. butter
5 small potatoes, boiled and diced
4 c. chicken bouillon or broth
2 c. milk
1 c. heavy cream
Salt and pepper, to taste.

Sauté leek and onion in butter on low heat until golden. Add potatoes and bouillon and bring to a boil. Lower heat and simmer until potatoes are tender. Divide mixture into batches and puree in a blender. Return to pot and add milk. Heat through. Remove from heat and mix in cream. Add salt and pepper. Put in refrigerator and chill overnight.

This soup is intended to be served chilled. That said, it also tastes great heated (no-one has to know you just committed a vichyssoise faux paux).

CABBAGE SOUP

⅛ tsp. garlic salt
½ tsp. garlic powder
⅛ tsp. ground black pepper
16-oz. can red kidney beans
2 celery stalks, diced
28-oz. can chopped tomatoes, drained
28 oz. water (use tomato cans)
½ small head of cabbage, coarsely chopped
3 chicken or vegetable bouillon cubes
Fresh parsley (optional)

Combine garlic salt, garlic powder, pepper, kidney beans, celery, tomatoes, water, cabbage, and bouillon cubes in a large soup pan and bring to a boil. Reduce heat to low, cover, and simmer for an hour. Garnish with fresh parsley if desired.

DESSERTS/ BREADS

Winford

BANANA CREAM PIE

1 large pre-made graham cracker piecrust

1 c. sour cream

½ c. milk

3.4-oz. package instant banana pudding mix

12-oz. container frozen whipped topping, thawed

3 medium bananas

Mix sour cream and milk. Add pudding package and mix until pudding mixture is dissolved. Add whipped topping and mix well, creating the pie filling. Spread half of the filling over the crust. Cut the bananas into ½-inch-thick slices and arrange half of them over filling. Spread remaining filling over bananas. Finish by topping with a last layer of bananas.

CHOCOLATE FROSTING

¼ c. milk

⅓ c. Hershey dry cocoa

1 c. sugar

⅛ tsp. salt

½ stick butter

1 tsp. vanilla

Combine milk, cocoa, sugar and salt in a pan. Over low heat, bring ingredients to a boil and allow to boil for 1 minute, stirring occasionally. Remove from heat and add butter and vanilla. Mix well and let cool.

PUMPKIN SPICE CAKE

For the cake:

- **3 c. all-purpose flour**
- **3½ tsp. baking powder**
- **2 tsp. pumpkin spice**
- **1 tsp. baking soda**
- **¾ tsp. ground nutmeg**
- **½ tsp. salt**
- **1½ c. sugar**
- **1 c. butter, softened**
- **½ c. evaporated milk**
- **3 eggs**
- **2 c. pumpkin**
- **¼ c. water**
- **1½ tsp. vanilla extract**

For the frosting:

- **8 oz. cream cheese, softened**
- **⅓ c. butter, softened**
- **3½ c. powdered sugar**
- **2½ tsp. maple flavoring**

Cake: Preheat oven to 325°. Grease and flour two 9" round pans. Combine flour, baking powder, pumpkin spice, nutmeg, baking soda and salt. In a separate dish, mix together sugar and butter. Add eggs, pumpkin, evaporated milk, water, and vanilla. Mix well. Gradually beat in the flour mixture. Pour into cake pans and bake 40 minutes. Let cool before icing.

Frosting: Mix all ingredients until creamy.

EMMY'S ITALIAN BUTTER COOKIES

- **1 c. butter, softened**
- **1 c. confectioner's sugar (10x)**
- **1 tsp. vanilla extract**
- **2½ c. all-purpose flour**

Preheat oven to 400°. Cream together butter, sugar, and vanilla. Gradually mix in flour. Chill dough for about 30 minutes. Roll into ½ inch balls and place on an ungreased cookie sheet. Bake 11 minutes. The bottoms of the balls will be slightly brown. Immediately roll balls in confectioner's sugar. Let cool and roll again until covered. Cookies can be stored for up to 30 days in a tin.

PEACH DUMP CAKE

- **4-oz. can crushed pineapple**
- **1 box vanilla cake mix**
- **1 stick butter, melted**
- **15-oz. can peaches**

Preheat oven to 350°. Pour pineapple and peaches across the bottom of a casserole dish. Spread cake mix on top. Top with melted butter. Bake 30 minutes.

ZUCCHINI HONEY LOAF

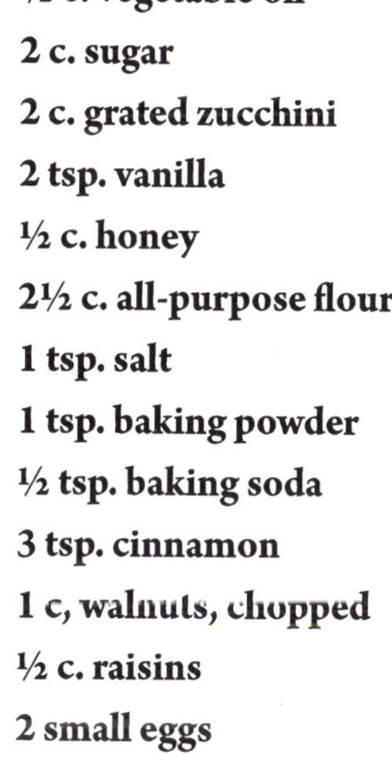

½ c. vegetable oil
2 c. sugar
2 c. grated zucchini
2 tsp. vanilla
½ c. honey
2½ c. all-purpose flour
1 tsp. salt
1 tsp. baking powder
½ tsp. baking soda
3 tsp. cinnamon
1 c, walnuts, chopped
½ c. raisins
2 small eggs

Preheat oven to 325°. Combine eggs, oil, sugar, zucchini, vanilla and honey. Mix well. In a separate bowl, mix flour, salt, baking powder, soda, cinnamon, and raisins. Add to zucchini mixture and mix well. Add nuts and mix again. Pour mixture into a loaf pan. Bake for 1 hour or until toothpick inserted in center comes out clean.

ANYTIME PLUM PUDDING

*Although this is generally a Christmastime desert, I think it's good all year round.

- **1 stick butter**
- **1 c. sugar**
- **½ c. candied fruit**
- **½ c. pitted prunes, chopped**
- **¾ c. raisins**
- **½ c. all purpose flour**
- **2 c. unsweetened applesauce**
- **1½ c. fine bread crumbs**
- **1 tsp. cinnamon**
- **1 tsp. ground nutmeg**
- **1 tsp. ground allspice**
- **Pinch of ginger**
- **1½ c. walnuts, chopped**

Preheat oven to 375°. Cream butter and sugar together; mix in applesauce. In a medium bowl, coat candied fruit, prunes, and raisins in flour. Add bread crumbs, cinnamon, nutmeg, allspice, ginger, and walnuts and mix well. Pour batter into a greased and floured Bundt or soufflé pan. Cook for approximately 50–60 minutes or until cake is slightly browned. Eat hot or cold, plain or with a hard sauce. Either way, it's sweet!

VANILLA HARD SAUCE

- **½ c. butter, softened**
- **½ c. heavy cream**
- **1 c. confectioner's sugar (10x)**
- **1 tsp. vanilla**

Combine ingredients and mix well. Spread over cake.

RUM BUTTER FOR ANYTIME PLUM PUDDING

- **1 stick butter, softened**
- **3 c. confectioner's sugar (10x)**
- **1 Tbsp. heavy cream**
- **2 tsp. rum extract**

Combine ingredients and mix well. Spread over cake.

BANANA WALNUT BREAD

2 c. all-purpose flour
1 c. sugar
½ tsp. cinnamon
6 tsp. salted butter
½ c. milk
1 tsp. vanilla extract
2 medium bananas, mashed
½ c. walnuts, chopped

Preheat oven to 350°. Combine flour, sugar, cinnamon, butter, milk, and vanilla. Mix in bananas and nuts. Pour mixture into a loaf pan. Bake 50 minutes or until inserted toothpick in middle of bread comes out clean.

BEVERAGES

Fix me a little libation, will ya honey?

FROZEN BRANDY MINT JULEPS

3 Tbsp. crème de menthe
1 c. vanilla ice cream
3 Tbsp. brandy
2 Tbsp. half and half
1 c. crushed ice

In a blender, combine all ingredients together. Blend and enjoy. Cheers!

COFFEE MILK

Kids love this…

1 c. milk
5 Tbsp. brewed coffee
2 tsp sugar

Mix coffee with sugar and milk and serve.

GRASSHOPPER 1

¾ green crème de menthe
¾ c. white crème de menthe
½ c. light cream (or to your liking)

Mix ingredients together and serve.

GRASSHOPPER II

2 oz white crème de menthe
2 oz green crème de menthe
2 c. vanilla ice cream

Mix ingredients together and serve.

MENUS

The following menus are samples and suggestions that are traditional in my family. All can be adjusted to make room for your favorite family meal or gathering. Only the foods with pages numbers listed next to them are actually in this cookbook.

CHRISTMAS EVE GATHERING

Artichoke Dip *(p. 18)*
Crab Dip *(p. 20)*
Maria's Beer Dip *(p. 15)* **with Beer Pretzels**
Potato Chips
Green Olive Tapenade with Crackers *(p. 18)*
Stuffed Mushrooms *(p. 19)*
Italian Wedding Soup
Glazed Meatballs
Italian Ziti *(p. 57)*
Lunch Meat Platter
Tortellini Yvonne *(p. 71)*
Sweet Potato Casserole
Blueberry Pie
Sweet Potato Pie
Anytime Plum Pudding with Sauce *(p. 90)*
Emmy's Italian Butter Cookies *(p. 88)*
High's Egg Nog (the best)

Make sure to have rolls/bread, pickles, along with condiments for the platter. Place little party dishes around the rooms and fill with peanuts, M&M's and your favorite Christmas chocolates.

This menu can be adjusted to the number of people you have invited. I always had open house and had anywhere from 15–50 attend.

THANKSGIVING DINNER

Turkey
Cranberry Sauce, canned or fresh (I use canned)
Stuffing/Dressing *(p. 68)*
Sauerkraut *(p. 64)*
Corn
Mashed Pototaes
Brown Gravy
Green Bean Casserole
Sweet Potato Casserole
Vegatable Lasagna
Biscuits
Pumpkin Pie
Manaschvitz Grape Concord Wine

EASTER

Honey Ham
Deviled Eggs
Vonnie's POEtato Salad *(p. 66)*
Green Bean Casserole
Rolls
Butter Lasagna *(p. 52)*

CHRISTMAS BREAKFAST

Scramlet *(p. 25)* **or Tofu Scrambler** *(p. 24)*
Creamed Chipped Beef *(p. 26)*
Bacon
Banana Walnut bread *(p. 92)*
Orange Juice
Pralines and Cream Coffee

RAVEN'S GAME PARTY

Diane's Bum Stew *(p. 44)*
Sherry's Seven Layer Dip *(p. 21)*
Maria's Beer Dip with Beer Pretzels *(p. 15)*
BYOL—Bring Your Own Libations

ORIOLES' GAME PARTY

BBQ Chicken Wings
Utz & Dip *(p. 15)*
Vonnie's POEtato Salad *(p. 66)*
Crab Pretzel *(p. 20)*
Burgers on the Grill

SOCIAL GATHERING

Thank you for purchasing *Baltimore Bites: A Taste from Home* and for contributing to animal welfare. I hope you have enjoyed the book as much as I have enjoyed serving the foods in the book over the years.

Your feedback is important to me. Feel free to contact me at **v52publications@gmail.com** to place additional orders and/or to let me know your personal experience using *Baltimore Bites*. All feedback is welcome. All reviews posted on Amazon are greatly appreciated. Thank you and God bless.

Vonna

"Unleash the cook in you"

CPSIA information can be obtained
at www.ICGtesting.com
Printed in the USA
LVIC04n1140291014
411057LV00008B/15